Good Seasons

SALAD DRESSING MIX

GOOD RECIPES WITH GOOD SEASONS

SMITHMARK

INTRODUCTION

Whether you are fixing a simple side salad or something special, Good Seasons salad dressing gives a fresh approach to almost any recipe.

Because you make it fresh, Good Seasons salad dressing mix has the taste of homemade yet the convenience of bottled dressing. We do all the expert blending of herbs, spices, even bits of vegetables and put them in each packet of Good Seasons salad dressing mix. You add the oil, vinegar and water. Then, to make it really easy, we give you a cruet so you can have great-tasting homemade salad dressing, fresh, anytime.

The Good Seasons tradition of freshness goes back a long time. Years ago, Robert Kreis, the chef at the famous Brown Derby restaurant in Los Angeles, became known for his salads and salad dressing. He became so well known, in fact, that patrons asked to buy his salad dressing. Rather than reveal his recipe, Chef Kreis packaged the dry ingredients and gave his customers an empty olive oil bottle on which he drew lines to indicate the amounts of oil, vinegar and water to add. Later, he sold his salad dressing business – including the idea for the free cruet – to us.

Good Seasons is still just as dedicated to freshness as was Chef Kreis. We refuse to add preservatives or artificial flavors. We still pay close attention to our recipe for blending spices and seasonings so each packet of Good Seasons salad dressing mix achieves the right marriage of mellow yet tangy flavor when combined with oil, vinegar and water.

As many creative cooks have learned, Good Seasons is not just for salads. Customize the dressing with various oils (try olive, sesame, walnut or any other variety) and different vinegars (such as red wine, balsamic or tarragon). You can even substitute wine or fruit juice for all or part of the water. Good Seasons can be as individual as your taste and as flexible as the ingredients in your cupboard.

And, Good Seasons is not just for dressing leafy greens. Use it as a vinaigrette over the market's or the garden's freshest produce, as a convenient and tangy marinade for meats, fish or poultry or as a flavorful ingredient for other menu items. Whether you are fixing dinner for family or entertaining friends for the holidays, here are 30 of our best-tasting recipes to give a fresh approach to everything you make, from appetizers to main dishes.

CLB 2600
©1992 Colour Library Books Ltd, Godalming, Surrey, England.
© Recipes Kraft General Foods Inc. 1992
All rights reserved.
This edition published 1992 by
SMITHMARK Publishers Inc., 112 Madison Avenue, New York, NY 10016.
Printed and bound in singapore.
ISBN 0 8317 3970 3

SMITHMARK books are available for bulk sales promotion and premium use. For details write or telephone the Manager of Special Sales, SMITHMARK Publishers Inc., 112 Madison Avenue, New York, NY 10016. (212) 532-6600.

SALAD DRESSING MIX

Good Seasons is a registered trademark of Kraft General Foods Inc.

POLYNESIAN TURKEY SALAD

Serves 6

This delightfully exotic salad is sure to please all your guests.

---

1 envelope GOOD SEASONS® Lite Italian Reduced Calorie Salad Dressing Mix
½ cup canned unsweetened pineapple juice
1 tbsp. soy sauce
1 tsp. finely minced fresh ginger
8 oz. snow peas
1 pound cooked turkey, cut into thin strips (3 cups)
1 cup diagonally sliced celery
1 (8 oz.) can sliced water chestnuts, drained
1 medium red pepper, seeded and cut into thin strips
1 cup sliced fresh pineapple
1 tbsp. toasted sesame seed

STEP 2

2. Blanch snow peas in boiling water for 30 seconds, drain and cool under cold tap water.

3. Combine snow peas, turkey, celery, water chestnuts and red pepper.

STEP 1

1. Prepare salad dressing mix as directed on package, substituting pineapple juice for the water and adding soy sauce and ginger.

STEP 4

4. Add dressing, toss gently and chill.

5. Add pineapple just before serving.

6. Serve in hollowed pineapple shell or on lettuce-lined salad plates, if desired. Sprinkle with sesame seed.

Cook's Notes

TIME: Preparation takes 10 minutes.

CREAMY DRESSING AND DIP

Liven up your salads with these delicious dressings. Or use them as a dip for crudites, crackers or chips.

1 cup mayonnaise
1 cup sour cream or plain yogurt
1 envelope GOOD SEASONS® Salad Dressing Mix, any flavor

Preparing the basic dip

For a classic dressing, blend ingredients. Chill at least 1 hour. Use as dressing for salads, as a dip or topping for vegetables and sandwiches.

For a creamy Vegetable Dip, prepare Creamy Dressing and Dip as directed, using GOOD SEASONS® Classic Dill Salad Dressing Mix. Blend in 1 (10 oz.) package thawed and drained BIRDS EYE® Chopped Broccoli which has been finely chopped in the food processor.

To make a delicious Clam Dip, prepare Creamy Dressing and Dip as directed, and add 2 (6½ oz.) cans drained minced clams and ¼ cup chopped green pepper.

For a Spinach and Bacon Dip, prepare Creamy Dressing and Dip as directed, adding 1 (10 oz.) package thawed and drained BIRDS EYE® Chopped Spinach, ½ cup mushrooms and ¼ cup bacon bits.

Adding spinach and bacon

To make an Avocado Dip, prepare Creamy Dressing and Dip as directed, adding 1 mashed avocado, ½ cup chopped onion, ¼ teaspoon hot pepper sauce and ½ cup diced tomato. Serve with tortilla chips or vegetables.

Adding the avocado

Cook's Notes

TIME: Preparation takes 10 minutes, chilling takes 1 hour.

VEGETABLE BITES

Makes about 2 cups

A whole range of colorful vegetables bring this tasty dish to life.

1 (8 oz.) package cream cheese, softened
1 envelope GOOD SEASONS® Italian Salad
    Dressing Mix
¼ cup Dijon-style mustard
¾ cup sour cream
Assorted vegetables such as:
    Red or green pepper pieces
    Halved cherry tomatoes
    Cucumber or carrot slices
    Blanched snow pea pods
    Belgian Endive
    Celery Stalks

STEP 2

2. Beat until smooth and creamy.

3. Chill 30 minutes or until slightly firm.

4. Spoon or pipe with pastry tube onto vegetables.

STEP 1

1. Combine all ingredients except vegetables in a bowl.

STEP 4

Cook's Notes

🕒 TIME: Preparation takes 15 minutes, chilling takes 30 minutes.

❓ VARIATION: Use a mix of your favorite vegetables, or whatever you have on hand.

SALMON PÂTÉ

Makes 1⅔ cups

This classic appetizer is always a guaranteed success.

1 (7¾ oz.) can red salmon, drained and flaked
1 envelope GOOD SEASONS® Italian Salad
    Dressing Mix
1 (8 oz.) package cream cheese, softened
⅓ cup chopped peeled cucumber

STEP 2

pan which has been lined with plastic wrap. Chill
at least 1 hour.

STEP 1

1. Combine all ingredients in food processor;
process just until smooth.
2. Spoon into small bowl or 5½ x 3¼-inch loaf

STEP 3

3. Unmold and serve with crackers or sliced
cucumber and parsley, if desired.

Cook's Notes

🕐 TIME: Preparation takes 5 minutes,
chilling takes 1 hour.

▢ SERVING IDEA: Treat a friend to this
special dish for lunch.

CHEESE TWISTS

Makes about 3½ dozen

Just watch these tasty bites disappear at your next party.

---

1 (10 oz.) package pie crust mix
1 envelope GOOD SEASONS® Salad Dressing Mix, any flavor except No Oil Italian, Buttermilk Farm Style or Ranch
1 cup shredded cheddar cheese
4 tbsps. (approx.) cold water

---

1. Combine pie crust mix and salad dressing mix.

STEP 2

2. Lightly cut in cheese with a fork or pastry blender.

3. Sprinkle in water, a small amount at a time, mixing lightly until particles cling together when pastry is pressed into a ball.

4. Cover with damp cloth and let stand a few minutes.

STEP 5

5. Roll out pastry very thin (⅛-inch thick) on lightly floured board.

6. Cut into 4 x ¾-inch strips.

STEP 7

7. Carefully twist each strip and place on ungreased baking sheets. Bake at 450°F. for about 6 minutes or until lightly browned.

Cook's Notes

⌛ TIME: Preparation takes 15 to 20 minutes, cooking takes 6 minutes.

◯ SERVING IDEA: Kids are wild about these.

HOT CHICKEN WINGS
Serves 4

Kids and adults alike will love these enticing chicken wings.

1½ envelopes GOOD SEASONS® Italian Salad
    Dressing Mix
½ cup butter or margarine, melted
2 tsps. hot pepper sauce
2 pounds chicken wings, separated at joints and
    tips discarded
¼ cup sour cream
¼ cup mayonnaise
¼ cup milk
½ envelope GOOD SEASONS® Italian Salad
    Dressing Mix
1 tsp. hot pepper sauce
4 oz. bleu cheese, crumbled
Chopped parsley to garnish

1. Combine 1½ envelopes salad dressing mix, butter and 2 teaspoons hot pepper sauce. Measure ¼ cup of the mixture and reserve.

STEP 2

2. Place chicken wings in shallow dish. Pour remaining dressing mixture over chicken and toss to coat well. Let stand 15 minutes.

STEP 3

3. Meanwhile, combine sour cream, mayonnaise, milk, ½ envelope salad dressing mix and 1 teaspoon hot pepper sauce; mix well. Stir in bleu cheese. Cover and chill.

STEP 4

4. Place chicken wings on rack of broiler pan; brush with dressing remaining in dish. Broil 15 minutes or until golden brown, turning frequently and brushing with dressing mixture.

5. Spoon reserved dressing mixture over chicken wings. Serve with bleu cheese sauce garnished with chopped parsley.

Cook's Notes

🕐 TIME: Preparation takes 15 minutes, marinating takes 15 minutes and cooking takes 15 minutes.

⊙ SERVING IDEA: Serve these tasty chicken wings with a salad and crusty bread for the perfect light meal.

GAZPACHO

Serves 10

Summer wouldn't be the same without this all-time classic.

1 envelope GOOD SEASONS® Italian or Mild
    Italian Salad Dressing Mix
2 tbsps. vinegar
2 tbsps. olive oil
3 cups tomato juice
Dash of hot pepper sauce (optional)
2 cups finely chopped peeled tomatoes
1 cup finely chopped onions
1 cup finely chopped celery
½ cup finely chopped green pepper
1 cup finely chopped peeled cucumber
Croutons for garnish (optional)

1. Combine salad dressing mix, vinegar and oil in a large bowl; stir in tomato juice and hot pepper sauce.

STEP 2

2. Add vegetables and mix well.

3. Cover and chill at least 3 hours or overnight.

STEP 4

4. Serve in chilled cups or bowls. Top with croutons, if desired.

STEP 1

Cook's Notes

🕐 TIME: Preparation takes 25 minutes and chilling takes 3 hours – overnight.

👨‍🍳 COOK'S TIP: Vegetables may be cut into large chunks and chopped in blender or food processor, following manufacturer's directions.

HAM CHOWDER
Serves 8

A hearty soup perfect for those cold winter nights.

1 pound cooked ham or smoked shoulder butt,
    diced
1 cup chopped onions
2 cups sliced potatoes
⅔ cup sliced carrots
1 tbsp. butter or margarine
2 cups water
1 envelope GOOD SEASONS® Buttermilk Farm
    Style or Ranch Salad Dressing Mix
2 cups milk
Chopped parsley to garnish

STEP 3

3. Meanwhile, combine salad dressing mix and milk, mixing thoroughly.

STEP 1

1. Sauté ham, onions, potatoes and carrots in butter in large pan until vegetables are tender, about 6 minutes.

2. Add water. Bring to boil; reduce heat, cover and simmer for 15 minutes.

STEP 4

4. Stir into ham and vegetables.

5. Bring to boil; reduce heat, cover and simmer for 5 minutes.

6. Sprinkle with chopped parsley, if desired.

Cook's Notes

🕓 TIME: Preparation takes 10 minutes, cooking takes 25 minutes.

✳ FREEZING: Chowder may be frozen. To thaw, place in saucepan and heat over low heat, stirring constantly.

❓ VARIATION: To prepare vegetables in food processor, chop 2 medium onions, cut in quarters. Change blade and slice 2 medium potatoes, cut in quarters and 2 medium carrots, cut in chunks.

MEDITERRANEAN-STYLE PITA BURGERS

Serves 6

A delightful mix of flavors makes this a meal to remember.

---

1 envelope GOOD SEASONS® Ranch Style Salad
    Dressing Mix
1 cup mayonnaise
1 (8 oz.) container plain yogurt
½ small head iceberg lettuce, chopped into bite
    size pieces
1 small onion, chopped
1 medium tomato, chopped
1 cucumber, seeded and chopped
1 envelope GOOD SEASONS® Classic Herb Salad
    Dressing Mix
1½ pounds ground turkey
6 regular size whole wheat pita bread
Alfalfa sprouts

---

2. Meanwhile combine lettuce, onion, tomato and cucumber in bowl.

STEP 3

3. Mix classic herb salad dressing mix with ground turkey.

4. Form ground turkey mixture into 6 burgers.

STEP 1

1. Combine ranch salad dressing mix with mayonnaise and yogurt. Beat with wire whisk or fork until smooth and creamy. Chill 10 minutes.

STEP 5

5. Pan fry or broil to desired doneness.

6. Serve burgers in pita bread topped with lettuce mixture, ranch dressing and alfalfa sprouts.

Cook's Notes

🕐 TIME: Preparation takes about 15 minutes, cooking takes about 10 minutes.

🔲 SERVING IDEA: These burgers are perfect for grilling outdoors during the warm summer months.

ITALIAN MEAT LOAF

Serves 12

An old favorite spiced up with the addition of tomato sauce.

1½ cups soft bread crumbs
½ cup milk
2 pounds ground beef
1 (8 oz.) can tomato sauce
¾ cup finely chopped celery
2 tbsps. chopped parsley (optional)
1 envelope GOOD SEASONS® Italian Salad
    Dressing Mix
1 egg, slightly beaten
Parsley to garnish

1. Soak bread crumbs in milk in medium bowl.

STEP 2

2. Add meat, half the tomato sauce and remaining ingredients and mix thoroughly.

STEP 3

3. Shape meat mixture into a loaf in shallow baking pan. Bake at 350°F. for 1 hour.

STEP 4

4. Spoon remaining tomato sauce over loaf; bake 15 minutes longer. Serve garnished with parsley.

Cook's Notes

⌊ TIME: Preparation takes 10 minutes, cooking takes 1 hour 15 minutes.

◯ SERVING IDEA: This hearty dish is perfect winter fare.

BEEF TACOS

Makes 12 servings

Give the family a mid-week treat with these popular tacos.

2 pounds ground beef
1 envelope GOOD SEASONS® Italian Salad
    Dressing Mix
1 tbsp. chili powder
2 (8 oz.) cans tomato sauce
12 taco shells

STEP 2

STEP 1

STEP 3

1. Brown beef lightly in skillet; drain off excess fat.

2. Add salad dressing mix, chili powder and tomato sauce and mix well. Simmer 5 to 6 minutes.

3. Spoon into taco shells, allowing about ⅓ cup for each.

4. Serve with grated cheddar cheese, shredded lettuce and chopped or diced tomatoes, if desired.

Cook's Notes

TIME: Preparation takes 5 minutes, cooking takes 10 to 15 minutes.

? VARIATION: Try substituting ground lamb, pork or turkey for the beef.

ORANGE-CHICKEN STIR FRY

Serves 4 to 6

Refreshingly different, this dish will spice up any occasion.

1 envelope GOOD SEASONS® Lite Italian Reduced
   Calorie Salad Dressing Mix
½ cup orange juice
2 cups broccoli florets
1 medium red pepper, cut into thin strips
3 scallions, cut into 1-inch pieces
2 tbsps. oil
1 pound boneless chicken breasts, cut into thin
   strips
3 tbsps. light soy sauce
½ cup walnut halves or cashews (optional)
¼ tsp. ground ginger (optional)
Hot cooked rice

1. Prepare dressing as directed on package, substituting orange juice for the water; set aside.

STEP 2

2. Cook and stir vegetables in hot oil in large skillet 2 minutes.

STEP 3

3. Add chicken; cook and stir 5 minutes.

STEP 4

4. Stir in ½ cup of the prepared dressing, the soy sauce, nuts and ginger, if desired.

5. Bring to a full boil for 2 to 3 minutes to thicken sauce slightly. Serve with rice.

Cook's Notes

TIME: Preparation takes 15 minutes, cooking takes 10 minutes.

COOK'S TIP: Remaining prepared dressing can be refrigerated to use at another time.

EASY CHICKEN CACCIATORE

Serves 4

Bring a taste of Italy into your cooking with this classic favorite.

2½ pounds frying chicken pieces
2 tbsps. oil
1 envelope GOOD SEASONS® Italian, Mild Italian or Zesty Italian Salad Dressing Mix
1 (8 oz.) can tomato sauce
1 medium green pepper, sliced (optional)
1 (4 oz.) can sliced mushrooms, drained (optional)

STEP 2

STEP 1

1. Brown chicken well in oil in 10-inch skillet.

2. Sprinkle salad dressing mix over chicken; add tomato sauce, pepper and mushrooms, if desired.

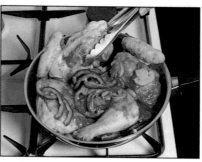

STEP 3

3. Cover and simmer 25 to 30 minutes, turning chicken pieces once.

4. Place chicken on serving platter and top with sauce.

Cook's Notes

TIME: Preparation takes 10 minutes, cooking takes 25 to 30 minutes.

SERVING IDEA: Serve with hot cooked pasta and a green vegetable such as broccoli.

SEASONED LEMON CHICKEN

Serves 4 to 6

Lemon complements chicken perfectly and here it is given extra punch with the addition of mustard.

---

1 envelope GOOD SEASONS® Lite Italian Reduced
    Calorie Salad Dressing Mix
½ cup water
¼ cup lemon juice
2 tbsps. oil
1 tsp. Dijon-style mustard
1 scallion, coarsely chopped
1½ pounds boneless chicken breasts

---

1. Combine dressing mix, water, lemon juice, oil and mustard in large bowl, mixing well.

STEP 1

STEP 2

2. Stir in scallions. Add chicken; chill 2 hours.

STEP 3

3. Bake at 400°F. for 25 minutes or until thoroughly cooked.

Cook's Notes

TIME: Preparation takes 5 minutes, chilling takes 2 hours and cooking takes 25 minutes.

VARIATION: Use 1½ pounds fish fillets in place of the chicken; bake about 20 minutes or until thoroughly cooked.

SERVING IDEA: Serve with fresh vegetables such as zucchini and carrots. Garnish with lemon slices and parsley.

LIME-DILL FISH FILLETS

Serves 4 to 6

Perk up an everyday dinner with this unusual combination of flavors.

1 envelope GOOD SEASONS® Classic Dill Salad
    Dressing Mix·
¼ cup lime or lemon juice
2 tbsps. water
⅓ cup oil
1 tsp. Dijon-style mustard
1 scallion, coarsely chopped
1½ pounds fish fillets

STEP 3

3. Add fish; chill 30 minutes.

STEP 1

1. Combine dressing mix, lime juice, water, oil and mustard in large bowl, mixing well.

2. Stir in scallion.

STEP 4

4. Bake at 400°F. for 20 minutes or until fish is easily flaked with a fork.

Cook's Notes

TIME: Preparation takes 5 minutes, chilling takes 30 minutes and cooking takes 20 minutes.

SERVING IDEAS: Serve with freshly cooked green vegetables. Garnish with lime slices and dill sprigs.

BROILED SWORDFISH STEAK

Serves 4

This popular fish is at its succulent best with a simple dressing.

1 envelope GOOD SEASONS® Lite Zesty Italian
    Reduced Calorie Salad Dressing Mix
3 tbsps. oil
2 tbsps. lemon juice
2 tbsps. water
1 pound swordfish steak

STEP 2

STEP 1

STEP 3

1. Combine salad dressing mix, oil, lemon juice and water in bowl.

2. Place fish on foil-lined broiler pan and brush with mixture.

3. Broil under preheated broiler 3 to 4 minutes, then turn and baste other side.

4. Broil 3 to 4 minutes longer or until fish flakes with fork. Brush again and serve.

Cook's Notes

⌞ TIME: Preparation takes 5 minutes, cooking takes 8 to 10 minutes.

◯ SERVING IDEA: Serve with broiled tomatoes and watercress.

BARBECUED SHRIMP

Serves 4

Always a favorite, this recipe can be adapted to suit almost any occasion.

1 envelope GOOD SEASONS® Italian, Zesty Italian
   or Garlic and Herbs Salad Dressing Mix
⅓ cup oil
⅓ cup red wine vinegar
2 small zucchini, cut into 1-inch slices
4 small onions, halved
1 red pepper, cut in eighths
1 green pepper, cut in eighths
1 pound (18 to 20) large shrimp, cleaned
Fresh chervil to garnish (optional)

STEP 2

4. Broil vegetables in broiler pan or a rack about 4 inches from heat about 5 minutes.

STEP 1

STEP 5

1. Mix salad dressing mix, oil and vinegar in shallow bowl.

2. Add remaining ingredients, covering completely with dressing. Cover.

3. Place in refrigerator and allow shrimp to marinate for 2 hours.

5. Turn vegetables, add shrimp and broil 2 or 3 minutes.

6. Turn shrimp and continue broiling about 3 minutes longer or until shrimp are cooked but still tender.

7. Baste occasionally with reserved dressing.

Cook's Notes

⌙ TIME: Preparation takes 10 minutes, marinating takes 2 hours and cooking takes 12 minutes.

? VARIATION: Barbecued shrimp and vegetables may also be grilled over a charcoal grill for about the same length of time.

VEGETABLE RATATOUILLE

Serves 4 to 6

Don't serve this just as a side dish. It's special enough to be served as a lunch or supper dish.

2 tbsps. olive oil
1 small eggplant, cut into chunks
1 medium zucchini, quartered and cut into 1-inch
    pieces
2 medium onions, sliced
2 medium green peppers, coarsely chopped
1 envelope GOOD SEASONS® Italian, Zesty Italian
    or Mild Italian Salad Dressing Mix
2 medium tomatoes, peeled and cut in chunks
3-4 tbsps. grated Parmesan cheese

STEP 2

1. Heat oil in large skillet and add eggplant, zucchini, onions and peppers.

2. Sprinkle with salad dressing mix; cook and stir about 5 minutes.

3. Cover and simmer 10 to 15 minutes, stirring occasionally.

STEP 4

4. Add tomatoes and cook uncovered for 5 to 10 minutes, or until tomatoes are tender.

STEP 5

5. Sprinkle with cheese. Serve hot or chilled.

Cook's Notes

🕐 TIME: Preparation takes 15 minutes, cooking takes 20 to 25 minutes.

❓ VARIATION: Add spicy sausages if you want a heartier dish.

PIZZA RICE

Serves 4

The perfect side dish or light lunch.

1 large green pepper, chopped
1 garlic clove, minced
2 tbsps. butter or margarine
1½ cups water
1 (8¼ oz.) can whole tomatoes
1 envelope GOOD SEASONS® Italian Dressing Mix
1½ cups MINUTE® Rice
1 cup shredded mozzarella cheese
½ cup sliced pitted ripe olives
2–3 tbsps. grated Parmesan cheese (optional)
Fresh basil and whole olives to garnish

STEP 3

3. Stir in salad dressing mix. Bring to a full boil.

STEP 4

STEP 1

1. Cook and stir pepper and garlic in hot butter until tender.

2. Add water and tomatoes, breaking tomatoes into chunks.

4. Stir in rice, ¾ cup of the mozzarella cheese and the olives.

5. Cover; remove from heat. Let stand 5 minutes.

6. Fluff with fork. Sprinkle with remaining mozzarella cheese and the Parmesan cheese. Garnish with the basil and olives.

Cook's Notes

⏱ TIME: Preparation takes 10 minutes, cooking takes 10 to 15 minutes.

❓ VARIATION: To microwave, combine all ingredients except cheeses and olives in microwavable bowl. Cover and cook at HIGH 4 minutes. Stir, cover and cook 3 to 5 minutes longer. Let stand 5 minutes. Stir in ¾ cup of the mozzarella cheese and the olives. Sprinkle with remaining mozzarella cheese and the Parmesan cheese.

SENSATIONAL SLAW

Serves 4 to 6

The refreshing taste of slaw is always appreciated during the warm summer months.

1 envelope GOOD SEASONS® Italian or Classic
    Dill Salad Dressing Mix
2 tbsps. sour cream
2 tbsps. mayonnaise
3 cups shredded red cabbage
3 cups shredded green cabbage
1 cup chilled halved seedless green grapes

STEP 1

Shredding
Cabbage

STEP 2

1. Prepare salad dressing mix as directed on envelope, substituting sour cream for the water.

2. Measure ¾ cup; blend gradually into mayonnaise and mix with cabbage and grapes in a bowl.

3. Chill, if desired.

Cook's Notes

L TIME: Preparation takes 10 minutes.

? VARIATION: Substitute 6 cups shredded green cabbage and 1 cup diced canned luncheon meat for the mixed cabbage and grapes.

CHICK-PEA SALAD

Serves 6

An unusual combination of ingredients which works very well.

---

1 (20 oz.) can chick-peas, drained
¾ cup thinly sliced celery
1 small onion, thinly sliced
¼ cup chopped green pepper
¼ cup chopped dill pickle
½ cup prepared GOOD SEASONS® Italian, Mild Italian or Garlic and Herbs Salad Dressing

---

STEP 1

Slicing onion

STEP 2

1. Combine chick-peas, celery, onion, green pepper and pickle.

2. Add dressing, mixing well, and serve on lettuce leaves, if desired.

Cook's Notes

TIME: Preparation takes 10 minutes.

VARIATION: Substitute 1 (15 to 19 oz.) can red kidney beans, pinto beans or lima beans, drained.

WARM GREEN BEAN SALAD
WITH BLEU CHEESE

Serves 4 to 6

Evoke a taste of the Mediterranean with this enticing salad.

⅓ cup prepared GOOD SEASONS® Garlic and
    Herbs Salad Dressing
1 pound fresh green beans, sliced
1 small red onion, coarsely chopped
1 (4 oz.) can pitted ripe olives, sliced
2 oz. bleu cheese, crumbled

STEP 2

STEP 1

STEP 3

1. Cook green beans in boiling water until crisp-tender; drain well.

2. Place salad dressing in microwavable bowl; heat on HIGH for 30 seconds or until warm.

3. Toss green beans with dressing, red onion, sliced olives and bleu cheese.

Cook's Notes

🕐 TIME: Preparation takes 10 minutes, cooking takes 30 seconds.

GREEK CAULIFLOWER SALAD

Serves 6

This pretty salad is both tasty and satisfying.

2 cups cauliflower
4 medium tomatoes, peeled and quartered
1 envelope GOOD SEASONS® Mild Italian Salad
    Dressing Mix
2 cups shredded endive or chicory
3 hard-cooked eggs, quartered
½ cup cubed feta cheese
Fresh chervil to garnish (optional)

STEP 4

4. Pour over cauliflower and tomatoes.

5. Cover and chill at least 3 hours to marinate.

STEP 1

1. Cook cauliflower in lightly salted boiling water 2 minutes; drain.

2. Add tomatoes.

3. Prepare salad dressing mix as directed on package.

STEP 6

6. Serve on shredded endive or mixed greens. Garnish with eggs, cheese and fresh chervil.

Cook's Notes

⏱ TIME: Preparation takes 15 minutes, cooking takes 2 minutes and marinating takes 3 hours.

B.L.T. IN A BOWL
Serves 8

A classic combination loved by all age groups.

1 envelope GOOD SEASONS® Italian or Buttermilk
    Farm Style Salad Dressing Mix
¼ cup sour cream
¼ cup mayonnaise
¼ cup milk
1 large head romaine, torn into bite-size pieces
    (about 8 cups)
1 pint cherry tomatoes, halved
½ pound bacon, crisply cooked and crumbled
1 cup (4 oz.) shredded cheddar cheese (optional)

STEP 2

2. Add lettuce, tomatoes, bacon and cheese, if desired.

3. Cover and chill at least 1 hour.

STEP 1

1. Combine salad dressing mix, sour cream, mayonnaise and milk in large salad bowl.

STEP 4

4. Just before serving, toss well to coat salad with dressing.

Cook's Notes

⏱ TIME: Preparation takes 10 to 15 minutes, chilling takes 1 hour.

❓ VARIATION: Use 2 medium tomatoes, cut into pieces, instead of the cherry tomatoes.

CHICKEN PASTA SALAD

Serves 6 to 8

A special salad which is sure to be requested time and time again.

1½ cups elbows, bow ties or medium shells
3 cups cooked chicken chunks
1 tsp. curry powder
½ tsp. salt
¼ tsp. paprika
¼ tsp. pepper
2 cups shredded romaine lettuce
2 cups shredded iceberg lettuce
1 large cucumber, peeled, seeded and sliced
¾ cup diced green pepper
½ cup diced red pepper
1 cup prepared GOOD SEASONS® Buttermilk Farm Style or Ranch Salad Dressing
Parsley sprigs

1. Cook pasta according to package directions; drain. Rinse with cold water and drain well.

STEP 2

2. Meanwhile, mix chicken, curry powder, salt, paprika and pepper.

3. Place romaine in straight-sided 2-quart bowl; top with iceberg lettuce.

STEP 4

4. Arrange layers of pasta, seasoned chicken, cucumber slices and green and red peppers in rings on top of lettuce.

STEP 5

5. Pour ¼ cup dressing in center of ring; garnish salad with parsley.

6. To serve, toss salad ingredients with remaining dressing.

Cook's Notes

TIME: Preparation takes about 30 minutes.

VARIATION: Add favorite vegetables of your choice to this salad such as mushrooms and cherry tomatoes.

BROILED SALMON SALAD

Serves 2 to 3

The king of salads – if you wish to impress your guests this dish is a must.

½ cup prepared GOOD SEASONS® Classic Salad
   Dressing
8 oz. fresh salmon fillet
½ medium zucchini, cut into strips
½ medium yellow squash, cut into strips
½ carrot, cut into strips
¼ red pepper, cut into strips
½ tomato, seeded and cut into strips
2 tsps. cilantro, chopped (optional)
2 cups salad greens
¼ avocado, sliced in six wedges

STEP 2

3. Toss salad greens with 2 tablespoons of the dressing.

STEP 4

STEP 1

1. Pour 2 tablespoons of the dressing over salmon in a small bowl.

2. Combine zucchini, squash, carrot, red pepper, tomato, cilantro and 2 tablespoons of the dressing.

4. Broil salmon, basting occasionally, about 5 minutes on each side or until done.

5. Arrange salad greens on serving plates; place vegetables in center of plate.

6. Top with salmon and fan avocado around bed of vegetables. Drizzle remaining dressing over avocado.

Cook's Notes

⌐ TIME: Preparation takes 15 to 20 minutes, cooking takes 10 minutes.

◯ SERVING IDEA: If economy is a consideration, you can serve this dish in small quantities as an appetizer.

PICNIC HERO
Serves 4

The perfect picnic treat, this giant sandwich is a crowd pleaser

1 loaf Italian bread
½ cup prepared GOOD SEASONS® Italian Salad
    Dressing
2 cups shredded lettuce
4 oz. sliced salami
4 oz. sliced ham
4 oz. sliced Swiss cheese
2 medium tomatoes, sliced

STEP 2

2. Spoon dressing onto cut sides.

STEP 1

1. Cut loaf of bread in half lengthwise.

STEP 3

3. Arrange lettuce, meats, cheese and tomato on bottom half of bread.

4. Add top half and press firmly. Wrap in aluminum foil.

Cook's Notes

🕐 TIME: Preparation takes 10 minutes.

⭕ SERVING IDEA: This is an excellent lunch time treat for the kids.

BEEF KEBABS
Serves 4

Everyone's favorite – kebabs cheer up every mealtime.

1 envelope GOOD SEASONS® Garlic and Herbs or Italian Salad Dressing Mix
1 pound top round or sirloin tip, cut in 1-inch cubes
1 large green pepper, cut into chunks
8 cherry tomatoes
2 medium onions, cut into wedges
8 small mushrooms (optional)
Watercress to garnish

STEP 2

STEP 1

STEP 4

1. Prepare salad dressing mix as directed on package.

2. Place beef cubes in shallow pan; add salad dressing.

3. Cover pan with aluminum foil and let stand in refrigerator at least 3 hours.

4. Dip vegetable pieces in marinade to moisten. Then alternately place pieces of meat and the vegetables on the skewers.

5. Grill over hot coals, turning frequently and basting occasionally with remaining marinade until meat is well browned and the vegetables are tender, about 10 to 15 minutes (or broil in oven in preheated broiler 3 inches from the heat for about 20 minutes).

Cook's Notes

🕐 TIME: Preparation takes 10 minutes, marinating takes 3 hours and cooking takes 10 to 15 minutes.

❓ VARIATION: Substitute 2 medium tomatoes cut into wedges and 8 small onions for the cherry tomatoes and medium onions.

MEXICAN SALAD
Serves 3

An adaptable salad which can be served with a variety of dishes.

1 (8 oz.) package BIRDS EYE® Deluxe Baby Cob
    Corn or Petite Kernel Corn
½ cup shredded Monterey Jack cheese with
    jalapeño peppers
¼ cup chopped red onion
½ cup prepared GOOD SEASONS® Mild Italian
    Salad Dressing
1 tsp. chili powder
1 avocado, sliced
Spinach leaves

1. Run cold tap water over corn in a strainer to thaw completely; drain and place in bowl.

STEP 2

2. Stir in cheese and onion.

3. Mix salad dressing and chili powder.

STEP 4

4. Pour over corn mixture. Chill 1 hour.

STEP 5

5. To serve, arrange salad on avocado slices and garnish with spinach leaves.

Cook's Notes

⤵ TIME: Preparation takes 10 minutes and chilling takes 1 hour.

◯ SERVING IDEA: Serve salad rolled in 3 tortilla shells or in fried tortillas.

SEASONED POTATO FANS

Serves 8

Here is an elegant and flavorful way to serve baked potatoes.

1 envelope GOOD SEASONS® Cheese Garlic, Italian, Mild Italian, Zesty Italian or Garlic and Herbs Salad Dressing Mix
½ cup butter or margarine, softened
8 baking potatoes or sweet potatoes

STEP 2

STEP 1

STEP 3

1. Stir salad dressing mix into softened butter; set aside.

2. Cut each potato into ¼-inch slices acrosswise without cutting all the way through the potato.

3. Using 1 tablespoon seasoned butter per potato, spread butter into each cut.

4. Bake at 400°F. for 50 minutes, basting potatoes twice.

Cook's Notes

🔲 TIME: Preparation takes 5 to 10 minutes, cooking takes 50 minutes.

🔲 SERVING IDEA: Serve with a fresh salad.

INDEX

Photography by Peter Barry
Recipes prepared and styled by Helen Burdett
Designed by Judith Chant
Edited by Jillian Stewart
Project co-ordination by Hanni Penrose